Houghton Mifflin Harcourt
Biology

Engineering Design Guide

Houghton Mifflin Harcourt.

Contents

Biology Engineering Design Guide

Lesson 1: What Is Engineering?

Engineering and science are closely related, and in fact, engineers and scientists often work together to solve problems of interest to both. Despite their close connection, however, the two fields have distinct goals. *Engineering* applies scientific principles to design and build products and processes that are useful to humankind. *Science* is the system of knowledge humans have about the physical world and its phenomena, based on observation and experimentation. Put less formally, science is a way to study the natural world, whereas engineering is a way to achieve practical solutions.

Both science and engineering rely on evidence and follow a structured investigative process that may involve data, mathematics, models, and computational thinking. Both fields involve asking questions and solving problems. Scientific investigations generally ask questions to develop explanations for phenomena. Engineering studies ask questions to help define a specific problem and find a solution. Both science and engineering are interrelated with technology.

Technology

In its broadest sense, *technology* is the application of scientific knowledge for practical purposes. Technology is a process as well as the goods, services, and products that result from that process. Some of the earliest technology included the use of simple stone tools to do work and two-wheeled carts to move goods and humans. Today, many goods are mass-produced in vast factories utilizing complex machinery controlled by computerized systems; similar systems control the transport of those goods across the globe. Technology, then, can be said to include all human-designed and human-produced solutions and tools.

Modern technology touches virtually every aspect of the human environment, from agriculture and manufacturing to computer science and the aerospace industry. Viewed that way, technology can seem like something that involves only "big things." Yet technology touches every part of your life every day. Look around your classroom. Just about everything you see is the result of technology. The notebook on your desk, the pencil in

Lesson 1: What Is Engineering? *continued*

your hand, the shoes on your feet, the cell phone in your pocket, the water bottle and snack bar in your backpack—even the backpack itself—were all designed by engineers and produced using technology. Without technology, life would be very different indeed.

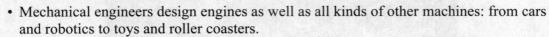

Types of Engineering

Engineering is a large and complex field composed of many branches and subspecialties that in turn serve many industries. Here are some examples of the types of engineers.

• Mechanical engineers design engines as well as all kinds of other machines: from cars and robotics to toys and roller coasters.

• Electrical engineers work in a wide range of fields, from power companies to defense contractors. They also design software and develop consumer electronics, such as smart phones and televisions.

• Closely related to electrical engineering is computer engineering, which helps develop computers, computer-based solutions for a range of industries, and of course, computer games.

• Chemical engineering serves a diverse array of industries, from large-scale production of industrial chemicals to pharmaceuticals. Chemical engineers also may work closely with environmental agencies to find solutions for recycling and similar problems.

• Civil engineers are critical to public works projects, such as building bridges, highways, and dams. Some civil engineers find ways to bring clean water to the public.

• Various engineering subfields in the life sciences involve solutions for producing food, pharmaceuticals, and biofuels, as well as protecting the environment.

The Connection Among Science, Technology, and Engineering

Science and engineering are closely interconnected with technology. The work of scientists brings knowledge that engineers draw on when designing solutions to solve a problem or meet a practical need. These solutions may then drive advances in technology that enable further scientific investigations. For example, the early achievements of scientists working with electricity led engineers to create power grids that brought electricity to homes, businesses, and public areas across the world.

The work of engineers, in turn, creates technologies such as microscopes, measuring instruments, and imaging software that scientists rely on to do work and conduct research. The development of the Hubble Space Telescope made it possible for astronomers to expand our knowledge of Earth's place in the universe, and brought insight into the origins of stars and galaxies. The James Webb Space Telescope will extend this reach into the universe. Even development of a seemingly humble instrument, such as a digital electronic balance or dissolved oxygen meter, can improve precision in measurements, allowing scientists to achieve more accurate results in lab work.

Lesson 1: What Is Engineering? *continued*

New ideas gleaned from science often bring a need for new technologies. These technologies, in turn, are developed by engineers and then utilized by scientists for further scientific investigations. The interconnectedness among scientific inquiry, engineering design, and technological development is reflected in the key roles each plays through the cycle of research and development.

The Impact of Science, Engineering, and Technology on Society

The interrelatedness of scientific knowledge, engineering solutions, and technological advances has had a profound and lasting effect on human society and the natural environment. For example, insights from scientific investigations have altered the way bridges are designed, crops are raised, surgery is performed, and machinery is produced.

Human society, in turn, influences science and engineering through its goals and expectations for technological developments. A range of economic, cultural, and political factors may drive decisions for improving or replacing technologies. Society also sets limits on the work of scientists and engineers, such as regulating the extraction of resources or in establishing acceptable levels of pollution from mining, farming, and industry.

Lesson 1: What Is Engineering? *continued*

A World of Engineering

Imagine a construction material that absorbs and destroys smog. Picture a robot that carries a patient and provides for other healthcare needs and comfort. Think about how solar panels built into roads could revolutionize highway travel. Engineers turn these and countless other ideas into reality. Those are just a few ways in which engineers use their science and math skills, and their creativity, to develop technologies for today and tomorrow.

Engineering in the Life Sciences

Engineering in the life sciences covers a range of areas, from medicine to agriculture and food safety, and from the improved design of prosthetics to improving methods of waste management. A few areas are described below. These and other specialties in life science engineering are discussed in more detail in Lesson 2.

Perhaps the most familiar areas of life science engineering are biomedical engineering and bioengineering. Biomedical engineers integrate general engineering standards with their knowledge of medicine and biology to design equipment, computer systems, and software used in healthcare. Some biomedical engineers focus on developing prosthetics and medical equipment. Bioengineers incorporate engineering principles with work at the cellular level. Nanodrugs, for example, are specifically engineered to transport and deliver medicine only to certain cells or cellular structures to treat diseases such as cancer. Both biomedical engineering and bioengineering may draw on aspects of chemistry, materials science, and computer science, as well as mechanical and electrical engineering.

Environmental engineering is a broad field that incorporates elements of biology, chemistry, ecology, microbiology, and Earth and soil science to solve environmental problems. Environmental engineers work to provide solutions for a range of issues, including recycling, waste management, water quality, pollution control, and the cleanup of hazardous-waste sites. Bioremediation is an example of environmental engineering. In bioremediation, engineers design processes that use living organisms to help remove toxic or harmful materials from the environment. An example of this is the use of oil-eating bacteria to clean up industrial oil spills.

Lesson 1: What Is Engineering? *continued*

The raising and processing of food is the focus of various branches of engineering. Agricultural engineers use basic science and engineering principles to solve problems in agricultural production. Some engineers may focus on improvements in farm machinery such as tractors, confinement systems for livestock, or storage facilities for grain and other crops. Other engineers may work to devise improved irrigation and drainage systems or better methods for soil conservation. Agricultural engineers need a solid foundation in biology as well as Earth and soil science.

Engineering practices are vital in the food-processing industry, where innovations in food storage and processing are critical for public safety. Engineers working in this field rely on a solid background in biology, microbiology, and chemistry to devise effective solutions to problems of spoilage and contamination.

Questions

1. How might the interrelatedness of science, engineering, and technology drive the development of a prosthetic leg for an injured dog?

2. Briefly describe the impact that development of a new technique to mine copper might have on society, and how society might in turn have an impact on further development of similar technology.

Lesson 2: Engineering and Biology

The human body has often been compared to a machine. Like all machines, its parts may sometimes need a tune-up or a repair. If the body cannot fix problems on its own, the work of engineers may be needed. Biomedical engineers use engineering to solve problems in medicine. Developing new methods of replacing body parts, delivering medicines to the correct location in the body, and improving designs for medical instrumentation and equipment are all part of their job. If the body's DNA is defective on the cellular level, genetic engineers may develop ways to repair or replace it. In the same way, Earth's environment may need repairs or a tune-up. This is the job of environmental engineers. They often design techniques such as bioremediation, in which they use organisms to solve environmental problems in waste removal, public health, and pollution of water and air. The sections that follow explore these three areas of engineering—biomedical, genetic, and environmental—in greater detail.

Biomedical Engineering

When a body organ such as a heart or kidney stops working properly and cannot be repaired, an organ transplant may be the only solution. However, there are far more people who need a new organ than there are organs available from donors. Because the body's immune system tends to attack materials that it recognizes as "foreign," an organ recipient must take lifelong anti-rejection drugs. Biomedical engineers attempt to overcome both obstacles by designing artificial organs. The process uses a patient's own cells and a 3D printer. A 3D printer is a device that makes a three-dimensional solid object from a digital file. By depositing layers of material one on top of another, engineers can build artificial organs.

First, the biomedical engineer designs and creates a scaffold, an artificial framework similar to the framework of a building under construction. The scaffold provides a structure on which stem cells will be layered and acts as a support for the new tissues that will grow from the cells. While the scaffold is being built, lab technicians grow millions of the patient's own stem cells. Using these cells as "ink" for the 3D printer, engineers deposit the cells in layers onto the scaffold. The cells begin to divide and join to form tissues. Eventually, an organ forms.

So far, engineers have built only artificial ears and hollow organs with simple structures, such as urinary bladders and tracheas. Artificial ears have been made with a collagen protein scaffold and cartilage cells. After three months, the cartilage cells had replaced all the collagen and filled the entire ear. When an artificial bladder was inserted in a patient's body and connected to his blood vessels and nerves, the bladder's scaffold gradually disintegrated and was replaced with natural tissue.

Lesson 2: Engineering and Biology *continued*

The building of an artificial organ is a slow and extremely complex process. Although organ engineering is still in its infancy, engineers are optimistic that artificial organs will eventually become plentiful. They look forward to the day when patients do not have to wait for years to get a new organ or worry that the organ will be rejected by their body.

In another biomedical research project, engineers are experimenting with prosthetic limbs that provide the sense of touch. Being able to feel objects is critical for performing basic tasks with the hands, and most commonly used prostheses do not have this ability. Now, neural bioengineers in Europe have developed a bionic hand with a sense of touch for a man whose hand had to be amputated due to an accident. The engineers connected electrodes embedded in the patient's arm to touch sensors built into the robotic hand. A built-in computer converted electronic signals from the sensors into a form that the patient's nerves could interpret. This sensory feedback could be felt by the patient as "touch." During training, he was able to control how much pressure to exert when picking up objects, how to distinguish between hard and soft objects, and how to identify the shapes of objects by feel. Although the "feeling hand" has had limited use thus far, bioengineers are hopeful that the system will soon be used by multiple patients.

Instrumentation is another interest of bioengineers, and they have designed many devices that have greatly improved medical diagnoses. For example, CAT (computerized axial tomography) machines use x-rays and a computer to generate cross-sectional views of human anatomy. MRI (magnetic resonance imaging) machines use radio waves and a large magnet to view body structures. Both machines are used to diagnose abnormalities in or damage to internal body structures.

Millions of people use many other devices that were developed by biomedical engineers. Hearing aids and cochlear implants for the hearing impaired, insulin pumps that deliver insulin to the bodies of diabetics without injections, artificial heart valves and heart pacemakers that correct heart problems, kidney dialysis machines for people whose kidneys have stopped functioning, and joint implants for people with arthritis are only a few devices that have enhanced and extended the lives of thousands of people. Many bioengineers think that people may not even have to visit a doctor for medical help in the distant future. Although robots and telemedicine are not likely to replace doctors, they will change the way doctors practice medicine.

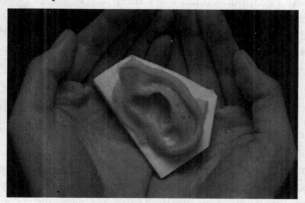

Genetic Engineering

In 1990, genetic engineers began work on the Human Genome Project, an enormous 15-year undertaking to identify and map all the genes in the human genome. They soon realized that computer technology at the time was not capable of storing and transmitting the huge amounts of data that would be generated. Biomedical engineers, computer engineers, and genetic engineers all worked together to design new technology that could handle the data. They designed and built robots that could do some of the lab work faster and more efficiently than humans could. And they even made improvements to the Internet.

Now, genetic engineers are using what they learned about the human genome to solve biomedical problems at the microscopic and submicroscopic levels. Working with biomedical engineers, they are designing miniature devices that are capable of delivering drugs and other substances to very precise target locations in the body to inhibit disease processes such as cancer. They also design gene therapy methods that carry normal genes into patients whose defective genes have caused genetic disorders such as cystic fibrosis. Some of these delivery methods use a virus to transfer the normal gene. Other methods use molecular tools to "knock out," or disable, a defective gene and then replace it without using a virus.

Genetic engineers work mainly in labs. The techniques they develop have been applied in diverse fields such as research, agriculture, industry, and medicine. They even have developed ways for bacteria to produce enzymes that are added to laundry detergents to remove stains. Some genetic engineers work with plants rather than with human patients. These engineers use molecular tools to rearrange DNA fragments in plants. Rearranged DNA can make a plant more resistant to disease, extreme weather, and insect pests. It can

also make the plant a more healthful food product. For example, rice is a staple food for many people around the world. Because rice does not contain vitamin A, people whose diet consists mainly of rice may suffer from vitamin A deficiency and even die. Genetic engineers modified the DNA of rice plants to include a gene from corn and a gene from bacteria. Both of these genes code for beta-carotene, a precursor in the synthesis of vitamin A. The modified plant is called Golden Rice. When eople eat Golden Rice, they take in the genes, which direct the synthesis of beta-carotene. The body then converts beta-carotene to vitamin A. Now, people who include Golden Rice in their diet are much healthier, and vitamin A deficiency is not as common as it once was.

Environmental Engineering

Environmental engineers use their knowledge of soil science, biology, chemistry, and engineering to protect people from undesirable environmental factors and to protect and improve the environment. Recycling, public health, waste removal, and water and air pollution control are all part of their jobs. Many environmental engineers are either civil engineers or chemical engineers who focus on the environment. Others have become experts in environmental law.

Lesson 2: Engineering and Biology *continued*

In the mid-1800s, a large-scale sanitary sewer system was designed and built in London, England, by the first modern environmental engineer. This project was important because the raw sewage that was being dumped into the Thames River was causing severe epidemics of cholera, a waterborne disease. Londoners have enjoyed a clean water supply ever since. More recently, environmental engineers have designed systems for municipal water and industrial wastewater treatment plants. They have addressed ozone depletion in the atmosphere, acid rain, climate change, and air and water pollution. An environmental engineering project might be as simple as designing a greenbelt bike path in an urban area or as complex as building a dam across a river. Environmental engineers must choose a location for the dam that has as little impact on the environment as possible yet generates enough electric power to serve the community. Soil analysis, water flow, and loss of wildlife habitats all have to be considered when choosing a site. Once the location is chosen, environmental engineers work with civil engineers and materials engineers to design the dam.

Environmental engineers in Italy have developed a type of self-cleaning concrete. Chemical components embedded in the concrete absorb energy from ultraviolet rays in sunlight and use it to break down pollutants in the air that would normally stain the surface of the concrete. By removing pollutants from the air, the concrete stays clean. More important, the concrete also helps clean the environment by removing pollutants. Engineers on the project have found that a road paved with the new concrete reduces the airborne chemicals that cause smog by up to 80 percent.

Questions

1. Briefly describe a project in which an environmental engineer and a genetic engineer might collaborate. What might be the tasks of each engineer?

2. Biomedical engineers have designed and built robotic systems that doctors use under joystick control to do delicate surgery. What are some criteria that a surgical system must meet? What constraints might there be? Suggest some advantages to robotic surgery over surgery performed without the aid of robots.

Lesson 3: Engineering Design Process

Engineers typically follow a design process to develop the best solutions to problems. This lesson describes that process. You'll discover that the steps in the process can be used to design solutions to problems in your everyday life, such as preparing food or planning a trip, as well as larger problems, such as adding lights to your school's grounds. In the the activities that follow this lesson, you'll have the opportunity to apply the design process to several engineering problems.

Like scientific inquiry, engineering design is a process based on a set of practices that can be used in flexible ways. In general, you can think of the engineering design process as having three main phases:

- **Define and Delimit the Problem** Clearly state the problem, describe the characteristics of a successful solution, and identify any factors that limit the solution.

- **Design Solutions** Generate ideas for possible solutions; select and test the most promising design solution.

- **Optimize Solutions** Use the results of testing to refine or improve your solution.

DEFINE AND DELIMIT THE PROBLEM

When tackling an engineering challenge, the first step is to clearly define the problem to be solved. To define the problem, you need to identify the characteristics that a solution must have to be successful. You can think of these characteristics as your criteria for success. You also need to identify any factors that might limit or restrict your solution. These limiting factors are the constraints on your design solution.

To take a simple example, perhaps you need a recipe to make a main dish for dinner. Your criteria for success might be that the dish tastes delicious and that it is nutritious. Some constraints might be that the ingredients cost less than $10 and that the recipe can be made in one hour or less. If any of the friends you'll be serving have food allergies, another constraint would be that the recipe not include any ingredients that would cause an allergic reaction.

In many cases, it is not possible to find a solution that meets all of the criteria perfectly while staying within the constraints. For that reason, you may find it helpful to prioritize your criteria so that you can identify the best tradeoffs between criteria and constraints. A useful tool for this purpose is a Pugh chart like the one on the next page.

Lesson 3: Engineering Design Process *continued*

CRITERIA	Maximum Value (1 to 5)	Solution A	Solution B	Solution C
Total Points				
CONSTRAINTS				
	Yes/No			
	Yes/No			
Which solution will you choose? Explain why.				

To use a Pugh chart to compare your solutions, follow these steps:

- List your criteria and constraints on the left side of the chart.
- List your possible solutions across the top.
- Prioritize your criteria by assigning a maximum value to each criterion, depending on how important it is.
- Rate each solution on how well it meets each criterion. If it meets the criterion perfectly, it gets the maximum value.
- Add up the points and indicate whether each solution meets all the constraints.

Design Solutions

After you have identified your criteria and constraints, you are ready to brainstorm possible solutions. Often you will also need to research the problem and explore the possibilities. You may need to study the details of the problem or different aspects of the systems that are involved. You should also review the solutions and processes that people have developed for similar problems. It can be easier and less risky to adapt an existing solution than to invent a new solution. For example, it is usually easier to use or adapt a recipe than to invent one. Existing solutions have already been through cycles of optimization, so many of the component problems and issues have already been resolved. The effects of the solutions, including unintended consequences, are already known. You might be able to choose the best of several possible solutions, you might adjust one solution to suit your problem, or you might combine parts of different solutions.

Lesson 3: Engineering Design Process *continued*

Generate or find multiple solutions or approaches. Use your knowledge and your research to imagine possible solutions. The first idea is not necessarily the best idea, so try to ensure that you have explored a wide range of possibilities. Sometimes an unworkable idea can lead to a better idea. After you have generated a good set of ideas, use the criteria and constraints to evaluate the most promising ones. The use of criteria and constraints can help you be objective, especially when evaluating your own ideas.

Once you have selected the most promising solution, you will need to test it to determine how well it actually performs. The results of your testing help you to learn more about your materials and the design of your system. Sometimes you may choose to test more than one solution and then combine the strong points of each design into a new and better design solution.

OPTIMIZE THE SOLUTION(S)

You can use the results of your testing as feedback to refine and improve your solution. Some parts of your design may have worked well, while other parts were problematic. Focusing your attention on these problem areas will help you troubleshoot your design and come up with ideas for making it work better.

Testing, evaluating, and refining your solution should be an iterative process. That means you may repeat these steps in a series of design cycles to arrive at the best solution. These cycles of optimizing your solutions are often where the most important work takes place as you refine the details and make sure all the parts of your solution work together effectively.

REFLECT AND COMMUNICATE

As with any process or skill, you will become better at engineering design as you practice it and gain more experience. Thinking reflectively about your design process is one the best ways to improve. You may find it valuable to use a notebook to record notes about your design strategies and thinking as you work on developing a solution. Your notebook is also a place where you can make sketches and diagrams to explore your design ideas and to refine details of your design as you troubleshoot your solution.

The notes and sketches from your notebook can also be a valuable resources when it comes time to communicate your design solution to others. The ability to communicate effectively is a valuable skill for engineers and other designers, who often need to explain and promote their solutions to customers or clients. They may also publish details of their design process in technical journals, so that other engineers can build on their work.

Activity 1
Design a Composting System

In this activity, you will design, build, and test a model for a composting system.

BACKGROUND

The billions of microorganisms found in soil are the world's most experienced experts at recycling. You may know of this process in nature as *decomposition*, *decay*, or *rot*. Microorganisms break down organic matter—once-living plants and animals, animal wastes, and dead leaves—to produce nutrients. The microorganisms use the nutrients to provide the energy and raw materials they need for growth, development, and other life functions. Most microorganisms need oxygen to perform processes such as cellular respiration, but some can get energy from less-efficient processes in the absence of air.

Carbon dioxide, nutrients, and a lot of heat all result from decomposition. Carbon in the form of carbon dioxide is released into the air, where it is available to plants for photosynthesis. Nutrients such as nitrogen and phosphorus are recycled back into the soil, where they can be absorbed by the roots of living plants. These recycled nutrients act as fertilizers that help plants grow. And when animals eat plant material, the nutrients pass into animal bodies, where they provide energy and raw materials for life functions.

The decomposition of organic matter occurs in nature, but what happens to the organic matter that results from human use? Most of it, such as grass clippings and other yard wastes, and kitchen scraps like banana peels and apple cores, ends up in landfills. These materials eventually decay, but it's a slow and inefficient process because there's not much oxygen or moisture in a landfill. As landfills fill up, more of them are needed to hold all our waste. There's a solution to this land-pollution problem that won't have such a large negative impact on the environment. It's called composting.

Materials

Use materials that your teacher provides or those of your choice.

SAFETY

- Wear safety goggles, gloves, and an apron at all times.
- Handle sharp objects such as knives, scissors, and nails carefully.

DESIGN CHALLENGE

Objective: Design, build, and test a small-scale composting system that successfully supports an aerobic, heat-producing composting process.

Composting is a waste-disposal technology in which organic wastes are decomposed naturally under oxygen-rich conditions. Composting reduces the

Activity 1: Design a Composting System *continued*

amount of waste that would be sent to landfills and produces a natural fertilizer that can be used to enrich garden soil, reducing the need for chemical fertilizers. You may be familiar with large outdoor composting systems that can recycle large quantities of food and yard wastes. However, you can also do composting on a small scale in your classroom using a variety of small containers. Your team's challenge is to design, build, and test a small model that successfully composts organic material.

DEFINE AND DELIMIT THE PROBLEM

Research the conditions required for designing and building a successful composting system. Consider criteria and constraints. The main criterion for your composting system will be that it must break down organic matter to form compost, as measured by heat production. Consider also the levels of moisture and oxygen, the balance of available carbon and nitrogen, the possible need for insulation to retain heat in the composting reactor, the need to avoid odors, and the availability of materials. Think about cost and safety as well. List the criteria and constraints of your composting project.

Criteria and Constraints

_____

_____

_____

_____

_____

_____

_____

DESIGN SOLUTIONS

You will need to think about both the design of the container for your system and the materials you will put in it. Research some designs for containers. Think about the needs for maintaining appropriate levels of oxygen and moisture and how you will meet these needs. Consider the possible needs for insulation and ventilation, and think about ways to prevent the release of odors.

Two common systems you may read about are made from soft-drink bottles and from nested cans (one can inside another). Evaluate these and all other designs you research to determine which one best meets the criteria of the problem and has the fewest constraints. If existing designs and the materials your teacher provides do not meet all the criteria with the fewest constraints, you may want to use different materials to design your own model.

Activity 1: Design a Composting System *continued*

Research some common types of kitchen and yard wastes, and then decide what materials you will put into your container. Do not include any animal products such as meat or animal fat because they attract pests and are very smelly when they decay. In general, you will need a mixture of "brown" high-carbon plant materials—wood chips, shredded newspaper, and brown leaves—and "green" high-nitrogen materials such as food scraps, grass clippings, and coffee grounds. Consider, too, the particle size of the plant material you use. How might particle size be a constraint? If you plan to add soil to your container, think about whether the kind of soil might be an important criterion.

When you have chosen a container design, sketch it in the space below. Decide on the best procedures for building and testing your model. Then, build your model.

Design Sketch

OPTIMIZE YOUR SOLUTION

Test the model in as realistic a situation as possible by measuring heat production in the container. Measure and record both the air temperature and the temperature of the compost mixture when you start the test and on each of two following days. If the mixture has reached a temperature of 40°C to 45°C within two days, composting has begun and the test is successful. However, if the temperature hasn't changed during this time, no composting is occurring. The test has failed, and modifications must be made. Remember, you can modify a design or procedure at any time if problems arise during construction and testing, but be sure to retest any modifications you make.

Record your test results on the next page. In the Notes section, record where and how any failures occurred. Also note what changes you might make to improve the success of a failing system or to trade less important features for those that are more important. Finally, explain how your design will address the problem you have been assigned.

Name _____ Class _____ Date _____

Activity 1: Design a Composting System *continued*

Test Results

Date	Time	Air Temperature °C	Mixture Temperature °C

Notes on Test

_____

_____

_____

_____

_____

_____

_____

Once you have a successfully working composter, continue to monitor the temperature in the container for two weeks. For accuracy, check the temperature every day at the same time. Make a graph of time (days) vs. temperature (ºC) in the space below.

Graph

Activity 1: Design a Composting System *continued*

Answer the following questions about your model system and its test.

1. Which criteria for container design and for the mixture of materials did you find hardest to meet? Explain why.

_____

_____

_____

_____

_____

2. Which constraints for container design and for the mixture of materials were most problematic? How did you solve the problems?

_____

_____

_____

_____

_____

_____

EXTENSION

Design an experiment that uses your model composter to test the effect of one variable on compost temperature in your system. For example, you might choose to test moisture content, particle size of compostable materials, or presence or absence of insulation. Perform your experiment. Communicate your results by writing a report or giving an oral presentation to the class.

Activity 2
Design Wildlife Corridors

In this activity, you will design, build, and test a model of a wildlife corridor.

BACKGROUND

Where would we be without roads? Think about how you used roads today, directly and indirectly. You certainly depend on them to get you where you want to go. But you also depend on roads for getting food to the school's cafeteria. Imagine how people and goods would get around without roads.

While roads are a necessity in any thriving economy, they can have a negative effect on the environment, specifically on wildlife and their habitats. Some of those effects involve collisions. In the United States, an estimated 1 to 2 million animals die each year from collisions with vehicles. This includes large mammals such as deer, moose, and bears as well as smaller animals such as rabbits, opossums, birds, turtles, snakes, and frogs. Some endangered species are particularly vulnerable to wildlife-vehicle collisions, including the Hawaiian goose, the desert tortoise, and the Florida panther. In fact, half of the deaths of Florida panthers are caused by collisions with vehicles.

Other impacts of roads on wildlife are habitat loss and habitat fragmentation. Habitat loss occurs when land and the vegetation growing on it are cleared to make room for the actual road and any shoulder space. Habitat fragmentation occurs when roads cut through a habitat, separating one section from another. As a result, large areas of habitat are broken into smaller areas, limiting where animals can find food, mates, and shelter. Habitat loss and habitat fragmentation also contribute to decreased biodiversity.

One solution to habitat fragmentation is to create wildlife corridors. These are narrow strips of habitat, often human-made, that link sections of habitats to each other. For example, putting in an underpass or overpass that animals can walk through allows animals to move safely from one side of a road to the other, reconnecting them to the rest of the habitat.

One of the more well-known and successful examples of wildlife corridors are the many overpasses and underpasses that connect habitats on either side of the TransCanada Highway in Banff National Park in Alberta, Canada. Each year thousands of deer, elk, moose, bears, and coyotes safely cross over or under the highway and have access to the entire habitat.

Materials

Use materials that your teacher provides or those of your choice.

SAFETY

- Wear safety goggles, gloves, and an apron at all times.
- Handle sharp objects such as knives, scissors, and nails carefully.

Activity 2: Design Wildlife Corridors *continued*

DESIGN CHALLENGE

Objective: Design, build, and test a model of a wildlife corridor that will allow animals safe access to habitat areas on both sides of a road.

Wildlife corridors that help animals move safely from one side of a road to another include underpasses, overpasses, culverts, and tunnels. In this activity, you will choose a habitat that is fragmented by a road and then design, build, and test a model corridor to allow wildlife access to the entire habitat.

DEFINE AND DELIMIT THE PROBLEM

Research more information about wildlife corridors, including the different types of corridors, their placement, and the materials they are made of. Then choose one of the following habitats and assume that a two-lane highway (one lane in each direction with a shoulder on either side) runs through the middle of the habitat.

- temperate deciduous forest
- temperate coniferous forest
- boreal forest (also called taiga)
- tropical rain forest

Consider the criteria and constraints for your model. How will you know that your model represents a successful wildlife corridor? What must your model include? Assume the types and numbers of animals listed in the chart are those that will need to be represented in your model for the habitat you chose. Think about the aesthetics of the corridors as well as any safety issues for humans near the corridors. Then consider the limitations of both your model and the corridor it represents. List the criteria and constraints of your wildlife corridor project.

	Temperate Deciduous Forest	Temperate Coniferous Forest	Boreal Forest	Tropical Rain Forest
Number of Large Mammals (e.g., bear, deer, wolf)	4	3	4	3
Number of Small Mammals (e.g., raccoon, fox, rabbit)	3	3	3	3
Number of Birds	2	3	2	3
Number of Reptiles	2	3	2	3
Number of Amphibians	2	2	2	2
Number of Insects	2	2	2	2

| Activity 2: Design Wildlife Corridors *continued*

Criteria and Constraints

_____

_____

_____

_____

_____

_____

_____

DESIGN SOLUTIONS

Research more about the habitat you chose and the types of animals found there. Consider what the landscape of your habitat will look like and the route of the highway. Choose the animals to include in your model. Then, generate a list of different types of corridors and their placement in the habitat. Depending on the size of the habitat, think about whether you need more than one corridor. Consider the following questions, as well as your criteria and constraints, as you evaluate solutions.

- What type of corridor will you build?

- Will you need more than one? If so, will they be different types?

- What will be the size of each corridor?

- What materials are used to build these corridors in real life? What materials will you use to build the corridors in your model?

- How will you represent the different types of vegetation and animals in the habitat?

- Some corridors have features to direct animals into the corridor and make it more appealing for them to use. How will you incorporate such features into your model?

- How will your model corridor handle drainage from rain or snowmelt? This will be the design feature that you will test in your model.

   Choose the most promising design for your wildlife corridor model and sketch it in the space below. Decide on the best procedures for building and testing your model. Then, build your model.

Activity 2: Design Wildlife Corridors *continued*

Design Sketch

```



```

OPTIMIZE YOUR SOLUTION

Create a procedure to test your model for proper drainage. You may want to test different scenarios, such as light rainfall, heavy rainfall, or melting snow. Collect data, make observations, and record your test results below.

In the Notes section, record where and how any failures occurred. Also note what changes you might make to improve the success of a failing system or to trade less important features for those that are more important.

Test Results

Amount of Water (mL)	Time It Took to Drain (s)	Other Observations

Activity 2: Design Wildlife Corridors *continued*

Notes on Test

_____

_____

_____

_____

_____

_____

_____

Answer the following questions about your model and the tests.

1. Which criteria for your model did you find hardest to meet? Explain why.

_____

_____

_____

_____

_____

2. Which constraints for your model were most problematic? How did you solve the problems?

_____

_____

_____

_____

_____

_____

Activity 2: Design Wildlife Corridors *continued*

EXTENSION

Design an experiment to determine if an actual wildlife corridor has successfully reduced a road's impact on local wildlife. What data sets could you collect and analyze to show the corridor's effectiveness? What equipment could be used to monitor the corridor and the animals using it? How could the results be used to determine if any changes need to be made to the corridor to improve it? Present your experimental design to the class.

Activity 3
Design a Safe and Healthful Animal Enclosure

In this activity, you will design and build a model of a chicken coop and run that provides for the health and safety of the chickens.

BACKGROUND

Picture animals on a farm. Chances are, your image includes chickens strutting around the grounds or sitting in nests of hay. Poultry farming usually is done on an industrial scale, raising chickens for meat and eggs as efficiently as possible. Recently, however, there has been resurgence in small-scale chicken keeping, not just on farms but also in suburban and urban environments. Many cities and towns allow a small flock of hens (female chickens) to be kept in backyards as long as the owners follow certain conditions such as keeping a coop a certain distance from neighbors. Usually roosters (male chickens) are not allowed in backyard chicken keeping, due to their loud *cock-a-doodle-doo* call. People raise chickens for many reasons, such as fresh eggs, to keep their food sources local, a desire for self-sufficiency, and to enjoy hens as pets.

Humans are not the only animals interested in chickens. These near-flightless birds are easy prey for many kinds of predators including some breeds of dogs, cats, coyotes, raccoons, foxes, skunks, opossums, snakes, hawks, and owls. Many backyard flocks have been lost because people did not realize what predators were in their area or how determined the predators would be to get a meal. At night, chickens are particularly vulnerable as they cannot see well and will often simply stop moving in the dark. If they are not safely inside their secured coop, they are "sitting ducks" for prey.

Many people attach runs to their coops to keep their chickens safe from predators while still allowing them some space to roam. Because the runs are connected to the coops, they too need to be predator-proof.

Materials

Use materials that your teacher provides or those of your choice.

SAFETY

- Wear safety goggles, gloves, and an apron at all times.
- Handle sharp objects such as knives, scissors, and nails carefully.

Activity 3: Design a Safe and Healthful Animal Enclosure *continued*

DESIGN CHALLENGE

Objective: Design, build, and modify a model chicken coop and run that keeps the chickens healthy and safe from predators.

Chicken coops and attached runs can be purchased in a variety of sizes and designs, but many of the ones sold by manufacturers do not ensure chicken safety or meet the requirements for their well-being. Your team's challenge is to design, build, and modify a model of a chicken coop with an attached run that will keep the chickens healthy and safe.

DEFINE AND DELIMIT THE PROBLEM

Research the type of nocturnal (nighttime) and diurnal (daytime) predators in your area that might try to get into a chicken coop and chicken run. Also research the space requirements and needs of housing six hens humanely year-round in your climate. Consider criteria and constraints. The main criteria for your chicken coop will be related to size and how well it will protect chickens from weather and predators. Also keep in mind such factors as ease of waste removal, ventilation, avoiding drafts, roost placement, nest boxes, ease of egg gathering, the ability of chickens to move and engage in normal chicken behaviors such as scratching and pecking for food, and the availability of materials. Think about cost and safety. Don't forget aesthetics; having an attractive coop can help the coop's owners stay on good terms with their neighbors. List the criteria and the constraints you anticipate for your chicken coop and run design.

Criteria and Constraints

_____

_____

_____

_____

_____

_____

_____

_____

_____

Activity 3: Design a Safe and Healthful Animal Enclosure *continued*

DESIGN SOLUTIONS

Brainstorm chicken coop and run design options with the members of your team. Discuss benefits and possible drawbacks of each design. Refer to the list you made of criteria and constraints. Be sure any designs you consider adhere to this list. Think about the chickens' need for ventilation and possible insulation, and consider how waste can be most easily removed and eggs most easily collected. Keep in mind predators that can fly, dig, creep through a narrow opening, and unlatch doors. Research online for other design ideas, and discuss how you could implement parts of those designs into your chicken coop and attached run.

When you have chosen a coop and run design, sketch it in the space below. Decide on the best procedures for building and testing your model. Then, build your model.

Design Sketch

OPTIMIZE YOUR SOLUTION

Test your model to find out how well it meets the criteria. For example, test how hot and cold your model gets during conditions that approximate your area's climate throughout the year. Test your model's ventilation. Test how well your model would protect the hens from predators. Record your test results in the space below.

Activity 3: Design a Safe and Healthful Animal Enclosure *continued*

Notes on Test

_____

_____

_____

_____

_____

_____

_____

_____

Present your design and test results to your classmates. After viewing all of the teams' designs, decide how you can improve your coop and run. What improvements can you incorporate for:

• keeping out all of the possible predators?

• providing year-round ventilation while not being too drafty?

• keeping the hens warm in the winter and cool in the summer?

• providing the hens with maximum space while keeping costs low?

Continue to modify your model until you are satisfied with its design. In the space below, record all of your modifications. Be sure to include both successful and unsuccessful design ideas. Explain how your design meets the criteria you set for your model chicken coop and run.

Changes in Design

Original Design	Modifications

Activity 3: Design a Safe and Healthful Animal Enclosure *continued*

Answer the following questions about your model, tests, and modifications.

1. Which criteria for the chicken coop and run did you find the most difficult to meet? Explain why.

   _____

   _____

   _____

   _____

   _____

2. Which constraints for the chicken coop and run were most problematic? How did you solve the problems?

   _____

   _____

   _____

   _____

   _____

3. Compare the original version of your design with the version after modifications. Explain what you chose to modify and what you did not, and why.

   _____

   _____

   _____

   _____

   _____

EXTENSION

The landscaping around the coop and run can either invite or deter predators. Research landscaping options for around the coop and run as well as within the run. Then sketch your coop and run and the landscaping that will best maintain a safe and healthy environment for the chickens.

Activity 4
Design an Aquaponic System

In this activity, you will design, build, and test a model aquaponic system for fish and plants.

BACKGROUND

You may have heard of aquaculture—raising fish or other marketable aquatic products, such as seaweed. And you may know that hydroponics is growing plants in water. But what do you get when you combine these two general methods of cultivating organisms? You get aquaponics. An aquaponic system is a closed loop system that depends on the interactions between plants, fish, and decomposers such as bacteria. Unlike a typical aquaculture system, an aquaponic system demonstrates the carbon and nitrogen cycles in action, thereby recycling excretions and other wastes, as is done in natural ecosystems.

Fish, like humans, release carbon dioxide (CO_2) through cellular respiration, which plants use in photosynthesis. Fish produce waste, primarily ammonia (NH_3), that nitrifying bacteria break down into nitrites (NO_2^-) and eventually nitrates (NO_3^-). Plants cannot use nitrogen in its atmospheric form, N_2, but they can use it in the form of ammonia. However, ammonia is toxic to fish and, in an aquarium, must be converted for fish to survive. Organisms use nitrates for many vital functions. Nitrogen is important in DNA formation, as DNA is composed of nitrogenous bases. It is also important in the production of chlorophyll, which is used in photosynthesis, and in the formation of amino acids, which are the building blocks of proteins. By using nutrients such as ammonia and nitrates in the water, plants clean the water, which benefits the fish. A successful aquaponic system allows both plants and fish to grow and thrive, and on a large scale can provide a lot of food relatively cheaply in little space.

Interest in aquaponic systems is growing because of people's increased desire to know the source of their food and reduce their ecological footprint (the use of resources to support their lifestyle). Aquaponics eliminates the need for pesticides, herbicides, and synthetic fertilizers, all of which contribute to water pollution. NASA and other space agencies are interested in aquaponics as a way of providing food during long-term stays in spacecraft and on other planets, such as Mars.

Materials

Use materials that your teacher provides or those of your choice.

SAFETY

• Wear safety goggles, gloves, and an apron at all times.

• Handle sharp objects such as knives, scissors, and nails carefully.

| **Activity 4: Design an Aquaponic System** *continued*

DESIGN CHALLENGE

Objective: Design, build, test, and modify a model desktop aquaponic system that can support the growth of fish and plants.

Learning how to design and build a small-scale aquaponic system helps build the knowledge base necessary for developing the larger commercial aquaponic farms of the future. Food security, providing healthful food in urban areas where it is not readily available, and lessening the impact of conventional agriculture on the environment are all goals of aquaponics enthusiasts. Your team's challenge is to design, build, and test a small model that successfully supports the growth of fish and plants with minimum additions to the system.

DEFINE AND DELIMIT THE PROBLEM

Research the conditions required for designing and building a successful aquaponic system. Consider criteria and constraints. The main criterion for your system will be the survival of plants and fish over time, which depends on the cycling of water and the presence of nitrifying bacteria. Consider also the need for a system free of plant and fish disease and without the contamination of other microbes that are often present in soil. Determine what species of plants and fish are most easily kept in aquariums when considering what organisms to use for stocking your system. Determine the minimum additions of energy, food, water, and other materials you anticipate to keep your system running smoothly. Consider cost, time, and space constraints. Write a list of the criteria for your aquaponic system and the constraints you anticipate in its design.

Criteria and Constraints

_____

_____

_____

_____

_____

_____

_____

_____

_____

| Activity 4: Design an Aquaponic System *continued*

DESIGN SOLUTIONS

After considering the challenges to designing an aquaponic system, research the details. Consider questions such as these:

- What containers will your team use for fish and for growing plants?
- What system will you use to move water from the fish to the plants and from the plants to the fish?
- What do the fish need in order to survive on their own?
- What can you add to the fish environment to encourage the growth of nitrifying bacteria?
- What medium will you use to support the growth of your plants without adding contaminating microbes to the system?
- What varieties of plants and species of fish will you use in your system?

Evaluate existing designs and consider the suggestions of your teammates as you determine the design that best meets the criteria of your problem within the constraints you identified.

Sketch and label your team's chosen design in the space below. Decide on the best procedures for building and testing your model. Then, build your model.

Design Sketch

OPTIMIZE YOUR SOLUTION

Test your aquaponic system to find out how well it meets the criteria. Add a few fish first, and check ammonia and nitrate levels to make sure that nitrifying bacteria are present and sufficient. When the nitrogen cycle is well established, begin adding plants to the system. Plant growth can be measured in the system, with control plants in similar light and temperature conditions but not part of the aquaponic system. You can add more fish to the system at this point. Record your observations and test results in the space below.

Activity 4: Design an Aquaponic System *continued*

Observations and Test Results

_____

_____

_____

_____

_____

_____

_____

_____

_____

_____

Based on your observations of fish and plant health and growth, decide how you can improve the aquaponic system's performance. Is there a way to reduce inputs without affecting system performance? Perhaps monitor nutrient levels and pH of the water. Take careful notes of changes and performance so that you know which changes were effective and which were not.

Continue to modify the aquaponic system until you are satisfied with its performance. In the space below, record all of your modifications. Be sure to include both successful and unsuccessful results. Explain how your design meets the criteria you set for your model aquaponic system.

Changes in Design

Original Design	Modifications

Activity 4: Design an Aquaponic System *continued*

Answer the following questions about your model aquaponic system and its tests.

1. Compare the original version of your aquaponic system with the version after your testing and modifications. Explain why you did or did not choose to modify your system.

_____

_____

_____

_____

_____

_____

2. Which criteria for the aquaponic system design did you find the most difficult to meet? Why?

_____

_____

_____

_____

_____

_____

3. Which constraints for the aquaponic system design were most problematic? How did you solve the problems?

_____

_____

_____

_____

_____

_____

Activity 4: Design an Aquaponic System *continued*

4. Proponents of aquaponics favor an increase in large commercial aquaponic farming operations. Based on your experience and research, what obstacles do you think this technology must still overcome before it can be widely used?

_____

_____

_____

_____

_____

_____

EXTENSION

Design an experiment that tests the growth of different types of plants in your aquaponic system. Do some types of plants grow better than others in this system? Research NASA's Veggie program and how it is helping scientists learn about human-plant-microbe interactions. Present your findings to the class.

Activity 5
Design a Nanoparticle That Delivers Medicine

In this activity, you will design, build, and modify a model of a nanoparticle that delivers anticancer medicine to a cancerous tumor in the human body.

BACKGROUND

One of the most exciting fields of science involves the ability to manipulate individual atoms and molecules. This is the growing field of nanotechnology. *Nano-* means "one billionth." Nanometers (nm), the units in which wavelengths are often measured, are a billionth of a meter (10^{-9}). It's difficult to visualize something at such a small scale. As thin as a sheet of newspaper is, for example, it's still about 100,000 nanometers thick. Yet nanotechnology deals with matter in the range of only 1–100 nanometers. Think of it this way: if a nanometer were the size of a marble, a meter would have to be represented by the entire Earth, to be on the same scale.

   Many products are the result of materials at the nanoscale, including stain-resistant fabric and composite materials used in bicycles and other gear to make them strong and lightweight. Nanotechnology has many applications in biology because many biological processes within cells occur at this scale. The double helix of a DNA molecule, for instance, has a diameter of 2 nm. The protein called hemoglobin carries oxygen throughout the body in red blood cells and is 5.5 nm wide. A virus may be 100 nm long. By applying their understanding of natural processes that occur at the nanoscale, researchers are able to design tools and processes at this tiny scale that have wide-ranging uses in medicine, the environment, energy, and other aspects of daily life.

Materials

Use materials that your teacher provides or those of your choice.

SAFETY

- Wear safety goggles, gloves, and an apron at all times.
- Handle sharp objects such as knives, scissors, and nails carefully.

Activity 5: Design a Nanoparticle That Delivers Medicine *continued*

DESIGN CHALLENGE

Objective: Design, build, and modify a model of a nanoparticle that delivers anti-cancer medicine to a tumor.

Scientists have been developing nanoparticles that can deliver drugs to targeted areas in the human body. These include drugs that fight cancer, drugs that help repair damaged arteries, and drugs that help treat eye disease, diabetes, and autoimmune disorders. In the case of anticancer drugs, using nanoparticles to deliver the drugs could reduce the side effects normally associated with chemotherapy. Nanoparticles that are used to deliver drugs in the body are not a "one size fits all" design. The design depends on many factors, including what drug is being delivered, to where, and for what purpose. Your team's challenge is to design, build, and modify a model of a nanoparticle that delivers anticancer drugs to a cancerous tumor.

DEFINE AND DELIMIT THE PROBLEM

Research nanoparticles in general, and then learn more about nanoparticles that are being developed to deliver drugs in the human body. Consider how you could make a model of a nanoparticle that performs this task. Think about the following questions as you work on the design for your model.

- How will your model show how the nanoparticle locates the tumor and delivers the drugs?

- How will you represent what materials the nanoparticle is made of?

- How will you represent some of the properties the nanoparticle has in order to function in the body? For example, how will the properties of your nanoparticle help it from being recognized as a foreign substance by the immune system?

- What properties will your nanoparticle have that allow it to function at body temperature?

- What will be the shape of your nanoparticle?

- How will you represent the precision with which the nanoparticle delivers the drug?

You must choose a scale for your model—for example, 1 nm = 10 cm. However, you must consider the size of any other particles you will represent in your model, such as DNA, RNA, or other cell structures. Your scale cannot be larger than 1 nm = 20 cm. Think about the materials you will use. Your nanoparticle should not be made of materials that are toxic to the body. You will not yet outline specifically how the nanoparticle will be constructed, but you need to have a general idea so you can anticipate any obstacles. List the criteria and constraints of your nanoparticle model.

Activity 5: Design a Nanoparticle That Delivers Medicine *continued*

Criteria and Constraints

_____

_____

_____

_____

_____

_____

_____

_____

DESIGN SOLUTIONS

Now you need to make decisions about how to construct your nanoparticle model. First, determine the overall shape of your model and what properties of the nanoparticle you want your model to represent. You also need to determine what materials you will use to construct the model. You might start by brainstorming various design options with your team. Discuss the benefits and possible drawbacks of each design. Look back at the list of criteria and constraints. Using your research, discuss how you could implement the real-life properties of nanoparticles used to deliver anticancer drugs into your model. If the materials your teacher provides do not meet all of your criteria with the fewest constraints, you may want to use other materials to design your model. Consider how you might use computer modeling to design your nanoparticle and explore its applications.

When you have chosen a design for your nanoparticle model, sketch it in the space below. Decide on the best procedures for building your model. Then, build it.

Design Sketch

┌───┐
│   │
│   │
│   │
│   │
│   │
│   │
│   │
│   │
└───┘

Activity 5: Design a Nanoparticle That Delivers Medicine *continued*

OPTOMIZE YOUR SOLUTION

After you have constructed your model nanoparticle, explain how the model shows how the nanoparticle works. Explain how the materials you used represent the properties of the particle and how it functions. These explanations are a way of testing the effectiveness of your model. Take notes as you work through your explanations.

Based on your notes, decide how you can improve your model. Do you need to change materials to better represent the properties of the particle and how it functions? Do you need to change the shape or scale of the model? Do you need to make any changes to improve how the model represents the overall function of the nanoparticle in the body?

Continue to modify and explain your model until you are satisfied with your results. In the space below, record your observations, modifications, and results. Be sure to include both successful and unsuccessful results. Explain how your design meets the criteria you set for your model nanoparticle.

Notes on Model

_____

_____

_____

_____

_____

_____

_____

_____

_____

Activity 5: Design a Nanoparticle That Delivers Medicine *continued*

Notes on Modifications

_____

_____

_____

_____

_____

_____

_____

_____

Answer the following questions about your model nanoparticle and its tests.

1. Which criteria for your nanoparticle design did you find most difficult to meet? Explain why.

_____

_____

_____

_____

2. Which constraints for your nanoparticle model design were most problematic? How did you solve the problems?

_____

_____

_____

_____

3. What additional properties might nanoparticles have that you were unable to address in your model? What additional resources might you need in order to model those properties of nanoparticles?

_____

_____

_____

_____

_____

_____

_____

_____

EXTENSION

Research the potential problems with using nanotechnology to deliver medicines in the human body. For example, some researchers are concerned about the toxicity of nanoparticles on the body. Some are concerned about nanoparticles being caught by the liver or spleen after they enter the body. Some are concerned with the general safety of their use and their compatibility with the internal environment of the human body. Are the concerns justified? Should more research be done to address these concerns? Support your opinion with scientific evidence.